CHRISTMAS FUN

Kingfisher

NEW YORK

KINGFISHER
Larousse Kingfisher Chambers Inc.
95 Madison Avenue
New York, New York 10016

First edition 1995
2 4 6 8 10 9 7 5 3
Copyright © Larousse plc 1995

LIBRARY OF CONGRESS CATALOGING-IN-PUBLICATION DATA
Robins, Deri
Christmas fun/written by Deri Robins: illustrated by Maggie Downer.
p.   cm.
1. Christmas decorations—Juvenile literature. 2. Handicraft—Juvenile literature.
3. Christmas cookery—Juvenile literature. [1. Christmas decorations. 2. Handicraft.
3. Christmas cookery.]
I. Downer, Maggie. ill. II. Title.
TT900. CR456 1995
745. 594'12 dc20 95-2454   CIP AC

ISBN 1-85697-567-3

Printed in Spain

CONTENTS

Holiday Treats

There are lots of different ways to count down to Christmas—one of the most fun is the Advent calendar, which has little doors to open on each of the days between December 1 and Christmas Eve.

Here's a holiday calendar with a difference—it has three sides, looks like a tree, and has a special treat in store every day. Why not make one as a surprise for your family and friends this Christmas?

You will need:

thin cardboard
24 tiny treats (candies, small toys, costume jewelry, pencil sharpeners, erasers)
cellophane tape
paints
needle and thread

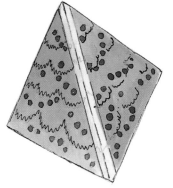

1. Copy this pattern onto the cardboard, and cut it out. Paint the triangles to look like the sides of a Christmas tree.

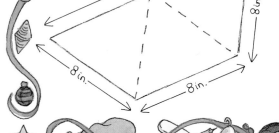

2. Fold along the dotted lines to make a pyramid shape. Then tape the sides together, as shown.

3. Draw 24 stars onto more cardboard, making them about 1 inch wide. Cut out the stars, paint them yellow or gold, and number them from 1 to 24.

4. Tie or tape a tiny present to a piece of thread. Thread the other end with the needle, and push it through the tree from the inside.

5. Thread stars onto your tree. Pull the thread to hide the present inside the tree. Knot one end to hold it in place.

6. Do the same thing with the rest of the presents and stars, spreading them evenly over the tree.

7. Hang up the tree by threading a final piece of thread through the top, and knotting it on the inside.

On December 1, use scissors to snip off star number 1!

5

Welcome Wreath

Wreaths are traditional at Christmas and they're a good way of welcoming visitors at this time of the year. Look out for cones and greenery during a winter walk—or in your backyard!

You will need:

base for the wreath: ask an adult to help you make one (see step 1), or buy one from a florist • small fir or spruce branches and cones • holly or mistletoe green string • red ribbon thin wire

1. To make a base, ask an adult to help you twist some garden wire into a circle. Pack clumps of

moss around the wire, and tie them neatly in place with string or thin wire.

Little brothers and sisters can make this simple paper wreath. You'll need cardboard and some green and red paper (you could use colored paper from old magazines).

1. Draw a ring shape onto cardboard, and cut it out.

Attach evergreen sprigs to the base with string or thin wire. Overlap them to face all the same way. You could add cones, cranberries, or tangerines.

2. Tear or cut leaves from green paper, and glue around the ring so that they overlap. Cut berry and cone shapes from colored paper, and glue to the leaves.

Finish by tying a big red ribbon in a bow at the top.

3. Cut a seasonal shape from an old Christmas card. Hang from the middle with thread.

Christmas Cards

Why buy Christmas cards when they're much more fun to make at home?

Printed cards

You will need:

thin cardboard
Christmas cookie cutters
thin foam or sponge
thick cardboard
glue
poster paints

1. Fold several pieces of cardboard in half, and put them to one side.

2. Draw around one cutter onto thick cardboard. Cut out the shape.

3. Lay the shape on the sponge, and draw around it. Cut out the sponge shape and glue to the cardboard to make a printing block.

4. Mix thick paint in a saucer. Dip the sponge in the paint and press onto the front of a folded card. Repeat to make many more cards.

5. You can also use your blocks to print matching patterns on envelopes, gift tags, and wrapping paper!

8

You will need:

thin cardboard—
about 10 x 8 inches
pencil
scissors
poster paints

1. Fold the cardboard in half, and copy the reindeer design. Make sure that the folded edge is at the top.

2. Cut out the reindeer, and cut along the line of its antlers. Press the head down slightly.

3. Paint the reindeer, or leave it white. You can write a message inside, or on the back.

Christmas Collage

You will need:

thin cardboard
scraps of fabric or paper, beads, etc.
scissors
glue

1. Fold the cardboard in half, and sketch a simple design on the front.

2. Cut or tear your scraps into shapes that fit your design. Then just glue them in position.

9

Trimming the Tree

People have been using evergreens to brighten up the home in wintertime for hundreds of years, but the idea of covering a tree with toys and baubles only began during the 1800s. Here are some special decorations to hang on the tree this year—they also make good presents after Christmas.

Christmas Tree People

3. Push the arms through the body, and attach by tying the joint with a piece of yarn.

4. Cut straight across the bottom of the doll. For a boy tie the bottom into pants

1. Wrap yarn ten times around your palm, and snip off the end (1). Tie one end (2), then tie again (3) to make the head and body.

2. Make another loop of yarn (4), and tie each end for the arms and hands.

(5). For a girl, make a skirt from fabric scraps (6).

5. Cut eyes and mouths from tiny scraps of cloth, and glue on to make faces.

Cornucopias

You will need:

colored cardboard
red and green paper
scissors
glue
thin ribbon
colorful candies

1. Cut the cardboard into squares, each about 6 inches wide, and roll the cardboard into a cone shape.

2. Overlap the sides of the cone, and glue them together.

3. Cut green holly leaves and red berries from the colored paper, and glue them to the front.

4. Punch a hole near the top of the cornucopia, and thread it with ribbon. Fill with brightly-colored candies and hang on the tree.

Window Dressing

The glowing colors of these "stained glass" windows will warm up even the frostiest of Christmas mornings!

Add an indoor snowstorm made from cotton balls, and you'll soon have the best-dressed windows in town. . . .

Stained Glass

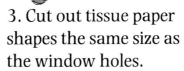

5. Glue the other piece of black paper over the top, and then tape to your windowpane.

3. Cut out tissue paper shapes the same size as the window holes.

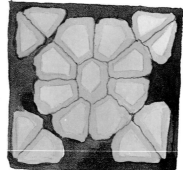

1. Pin or clip the pieces of black paper together.

2. Use chalk to draw this design on the top piece of paper. Cut the holes from both thicknesses of paper with scissors.

4. Glue the tissue pieces over all the holes in one piece of black paper.

A Snowstorm

You will need:

white cotton balls
white or clear thread
needle

2. Thread some cotton balls onto each length, leaving a gap of 2-3 inches between each ball. Attach to the top of a window as shown.

1. Cut several lengths from the thread, each about 15 inches long. Thread the first piece onto a needle, and tie a knot at the end.

Nativity Scene

Here's a beautiful model Nativity scene for Christmas. It's great fun to make, and a good way to remember what happened on that very first Christmas Eve, nearly 2,000 years ago. . . .

For the stable, you'll need:

a shoebox, or other small cardboard box
a handful of thin twigs
scissors
glue

▶ Ask an adult to help you cut any flaps off the box. Then lay the box on its side, and cut the top at an angle, as shown in the picture.

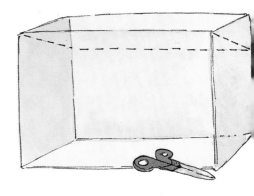

◀ Cut holes in the two side pieces, so that just a basic frame is left. Then take your twigs and brush off any dirt or leaves.

▶ Snap the twigs to the length you need, and glue inside the back of the box. Then glue twigs over the side pieces of the frame.

▶ Measure between A and B on your box, and break several twigs to this length. Glue them side by side to make a roof, and glue onto the box when dry.

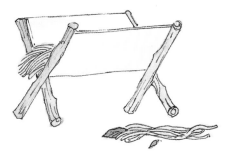

◀ To make the manger, just fold a small piece of cardboard in half, and glue two twigs in a crisscross at each end.

Making the Figures

To make the figures, you'll need to mix up some home-made salt dough. You'll also need some poster paints, and a little varnish to protect the figures.

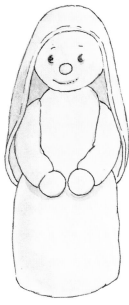

1. Roll a thick sausage from dough, for the body. Roll thin sausages for arms, with small balls for hands.

2. Roll a ball for the head, and a tiny blob for the nose. Press in a pencil to make the eyes and mouth.

3. Cut a thin square of dough to make the headdress. Drape over the head and body.

SALT DOUGH RECIPE

You will need:

3 cups flour
1 cup salt
1 cup water

1. Stir all the ingredients together until they're well mixed.

2. Knead the dough for about two minutes until it's really smooth and stretchy. Put it in a plastic bag in the fridge for half an hour before using.

4. Add any extra features, then stand the figures on foil on a cookie sheet.

5. Let them dry out in a cool oven (250°F), for about three hours. Paint and varnish them when they've cooled down.

▶ Make sheep from sausages and balls of dough. Roughen the backs with a fork before you bake them.

◀ Make angel hair by pushing dough through a garlic press. Glue on a halo and wings made from cardboard, and paint them gold.

The infant Jesus is made from a sausage and ball of dough. ▼

▼ Make a hole through one of the shepherds' hands with a toothpick before baking. Later, add a crook made from a pipe cleaner.

◀ This king has a crown and a beard made from dough (if the bits come off during baking, they can be glued on again before painting). The box is made from a cube of dough.

The Butcher, the Baker...

In France, children have some unusual-looking characters in their Nativity scenes. As well as the Nativity figures, you'll often see ordinary townspeople, such as the mayor and the butcher!

Dangly Santa

You can trace the shapes on these pages to make a little decoration or copy them at a much bigger size. How about making a really huge Santa to hang up in the hall?

You will need:

red, white, and black cardboard
scissors • glue
cotton balls
needle and thread

1. Trace or copy the boots onto black cardboard, and the eyes onto white cardboard. Copy the rest onto red cardboard, and cut all the pieces out.

2. Cut black and white cardboard to make the hands, belt, and buckle, and glue to both sides of the body.

3. Glue cotton balls to make the trim for the coat, boots, and hat, and for the eyebrows and mustache. Decorate both sides of the pieces.

4. Use short lengths of thread to link all the parts of the Santa together, and hang from the ceiling.

19

Christmas Bells

These beautiful tissue-paper bells fold flat after Christmas, so that you can pack them away safely until next year. . . .

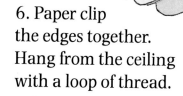

You will need:

two squares of tissue paper
thin cardboard
scissors • glue
paper clips

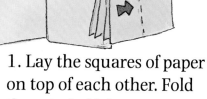
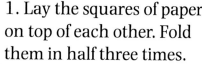

1. Lay the squares of paper on top of each other. Fold them in half three times.

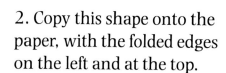

2. Copy this shape onto the paper, with the folded edges on the left and at the top.

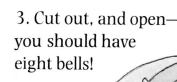

3. Cut out, and open—you should have eight bells!

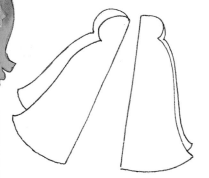

4. Cut out an identical bell from the thin cardboard, and cut it in half. Put these pieces to one side.

5. Fold each tissue bell in half, and glue the halves back-to-back. Glue the cardboard halves to each end.

6. Paper clip the edges together. Hang from the ceiling with a loop of thread.

No-Glue Garlands

Here are two fun ways to make colorful paper streamers—they don't require gluing, just a little cutting and folding. All you need is crepe paper, a pair of scissors, and a small piece of cardboard.

Paper Chains

1. Fold cardboard in half, then draw and cut out the above shape to use as a template.

2. Use the template to cut out at least 20 identical shapes from folded strips of colored paper.

3. Link together by opening them out and looping them through each other.

Cut - and - Pulls

1. Cut a long strip of crepe paper, about 35 inches long. Fold it in half twice.

3. Unfold the strip once. Pull the edges of the streamer, and watch it grow!

2. Make equally-spaced cuts along both long sides of the folded crepe paper.

Christmas Cookbook

The kitchen is often busy at Christmas, but you may be able to persuade the Chief Cook to let you make these special treats! *Always* ask an adult to help when you're cooking.

Christmas Pizza

You will need:

ready-made pizza dough (grapefruit size)
$1/3$ cup pizza sauce
1 green pepper
cheese slices
stuffed olives
a few anchovies • flour

Great fun for lunch, or as part of a buffet if you have guests coming over. . .

Before you begin, set the oven to 425°F.

1. On a lightly floured surface, roll out the dough into a circle. Grease a pizza pan and press in the dough until it fits.

2. Spread the pizza sauce over the dough.

3. Cut green pepper into thin slices, and arrange to look like a Christmas tree.

4. Cut strips of cheese for the candles, and halve the olives for the flames. Make the trunk from anchovies.

5. Ask an adult to put the pizza in the oven, and bake for 25 minutes. The dough should be crisp and golden brown.

Christmas Cookies

Use cookie cutters to make Christmas shapes to hang on the tree, or cut out giant shapes with a blunt knife....

You will need:

¹/₃ cup butter
1 egg
1¹/₂ cups flour
2 oz. corn syrup
¹/₂ cup light brown sugar
1 tsp. cinnamon
1 tsp. ginger

Set the oven to 350°F.

1. Sift the flour, spices, and baking powder into a big bowl. Add the sugar, and rub in the butter to make fine breadcrumbs.

3. Roll out the dough to about 1/4 inch thick. Cut Christmas shapes from the dough and, using a toothpick, make holes in the tops.

4. Lay the shapes on a greased cookie sheet, and ask an adult to cook them for about 15 minutes.

2. Beat the egg and syrup together, and add to the flour—mix into a dough. Place in a freezer bag and refrigerate for half an hour.

5. Decorate them when they're cool—use confectioners' sugar, 1 tbsp. water, and a little food coloring. Thread ribbon through the holes.

23

Snowballs

This recipe makes a blizzard of snowballs. There may even be a few left when your guests arrive. . . .

You will need:

1 cup white breadcrumbs
3/4 cup chopped nuts
8 oz. pack of cream cheese
1 stalk of celery
salt and pepper
dried coconut

1. Ask an adult to help you chop the celery.

2. Mix the celery with the cheese, breadcrumbs, and nuts, and add a pinch of salt and pepper.

3. Roll the mixture into balls the size of walnuts.

4. Put coconut on a plate, and roll the cheese balls in it to coat them. Refrigerate until needed.

Winter Warmer

This is the perfect way to greet someone who's just come in from a frosty winter's walk. . . .

You will need:

1 pint apple juice • 1 tbsp. concentrated grape juice
juice of 1/2 a lemon
a pinch of ginger
cinnamon sticks

1. Put all the ingredients in a big, heavy pan. Ask an adult to heat them until they're piping hot (but not boiling).

2. Ask an adult to pour into mugs through a strainer. Add a swirl of honey and slices of lemon, orange, or apple.

24

Christmas Crunch

A tasty snack to offer guests with their Winter Warmer, or to pack in a sandwich bag for a quick on-the-run outdoor picnic. . . .

You will need:

1 cup breakfast cereal
1/2 cup shelled peanuts
1/2 cup dried raisins, dates, or apricots
1/2 cup dried coconut
1/2 cup banana chips

Just mix together!

(Not only is this delicious, but it's a lot better for you than store-bought foods like potato chips or cookies. Try adding milk to the mixture for the perfect breakfast. . .)

Ambrosia

This delectable dessert is traditionally served after the main Christmas dinner in many South American countries.

1. Peel the fresh fruit. Ask an adult to help you open the canned fruit and chop it into chunks.

2. Mix all the ingredients together, and chill in the fridge for about an hour.

3. Serve topped with ice cream or whipped cream.

You will need:

one 8-oz. can peaches
one 8-oz. can pineapple chunks
2 oranges
2 bananas
1/2 cup flaked coconut

Perfect Presents

Make your favorite grown-ups happy this Christmas by giving them homemade presents! The ideas on these pages are so quick and easy that you may even consider going into mass production. . . .

Print-a-T-shirt

You will need:

plain white cotton T-shirt to fit your grown-up
fabric paints or pens (pens for outlines, paints for big areas of color)
paper • cardboard

1. Sketch out some designs for your T-shirt on the paper.

2. Push cardboard inside the T-shirt and pin it flat. Paint your design onto the front, and leave it to dry.

NOTE: Many fabric paints need to be ironed to make them colorfast. If so, ask an adult to help.

SECOND NOTE: It's just as easy to paint an apron, a pair of shorts, or a pillowcase!

Fridge Magnets

will need:

-hardening clay
ristmas cookie
cutters
poster paints
waterproof varnish
small magnets • glue

1. Roll out the clay until it's about 1 inch thick.

2. Cut out shapes with the cookie cutters, and leave them in a warm place to dry out completely. For small objects this will take about 24 hours.

3. Paint and varnish the shapes. When they're dry, glue a magnet to the back of each one.

Santa Bath Mitten

You will need:

your hand
thin foam or terry cloth
(red, white, and black,
if possible)
a needle and thread
a felt-tipped
pen

1. Use your hands as guides for drawing two mitten shapes on the foam, allowing an extra 1/2 inch all round. Cut the mitten shapes out.

2. Sew together, leaving the bottom open, and turn inside out. Cut the hat, trim, and features from extra foam, and sew to the mitten.

27

Christmas Games

Christmas wouldn't be Christmas without games!
Noisy games, quiet games, games of chance, and
games of skill—there's something here to suit every mood
and occasion over the holiday.

Santa's Sack

You'll need at least three
friends and a bag full of
noisy clanking things
(empty soda cans are
good for this).

1. One player takes the part of
Santa, while everyone else ties a
blindfold around his or her eyes.

2. Everyone listens out for Santa's sack,
and tries to grab it. The winner plays
Santa next time around.

Dressing the Tree

Any number can play.
You'll each need to make
a tree and six decorations
—cut them out of card-
board, and color them in.
You'll also need a die.

1. Number each of
your decorations from 1 to 6.

2. Take turns throwing the
die. So, if you throw a 2,
put decoration number 2
on your tree. The player
to put all their decorations
on their tree first is
the winner!

The Hidden Card

Any number can play. All you need is an old Christmas card for each person.

1. Each player tears a card into four pieces, and hides three of them around the room (you must be able to see them without moving anything). Give the last piece to another player.

2. The winner is the first player to complete his or her jigsaw!

Christmas Croquet

This game works best with two or three players. You'll need some cardboard, scissors, and a marble for each player.

1. Cut ten 4-inch strips from cardboard. Bend into hoops and number from 1 to 10.

2. Cut a seasonal shape from cardboard, and cut two holes for your fingers.

3. Take turns to flick a marble gently through the shape. The marble must go under each hoop in the right order. Whoever completes the course first wins!

Christmas Wildlife

It's great being outdoors on a frosty morning—unless you happen to be a bird. It's hard for them to find food and water when the ground is frozen, and many go hungry. By giving them their own Christmas tree, you could help to save their lives.

▶ Choose a tree in your backyard to decorate. If you only have a small yard, tie big sticks together, and "plant" them in a big pot.

▼ Spread pinecones with peanut butter, roll them in birdseed, and hang on the tree with thread.

▲ Make garlands for the tree: thread a darning needle, and knot one end. Thread on peanuts in their shells, cranberries, or millet.

◄ Chunks of coconut or corn can be hung up with ribbon, or try making holes in apples, and studding them with seeds.

► Don't forget water! Put some out in a shallow bowl, but well away from cats.

Spare a thought for all the trees that are felled each Christmas. You don't have to buy a cut tree—why not choose a living one, which will go on growing for years and years? Most pines and firs can be kept in pots. When they start to outgrow them, they can be planted outside.

After Christmas

Christmas doesn't have to end on December 26. Here are some things to do even after the day is over.

Discover how to be Very, Very Popular

. . . with the grown-ups, that is. Help with the household chores—and don't wait to be asked! (Remember, it's their holiday too. . .)

Christmas Collage

Make Christmas last longer by making a special collage. Use bits of wrapping paper, your favorite cards, snapshots, gift tags, party hats, tinsel, candy wrappers, party invitations —unless it moves, collage it! Glue to a piece of cardboard, or stick in a scrapbook.

Get in Touch

With a bit of thought and imagination, sending thank-you letters need never be boring. If you can't think of anything interesting to say, you could print some good-looking cards and envelopes (see page 8), and just add a short thank-you message.

New Year Promises

If you can't think of any New Year's resolutions, maybe your friends, brothers, and sisters will have some suggestions. . . Make a list of resolutions and pin them to the wall. Give yourself 10 points each week in the New Year that you keep them. Can you make it to 100?